Dear James,

I hope you find a few poems to give you pleasure.

Love and peace,

Stella

Colors of the River: Poems

Stella Ann Nesanovich

Stella Ann Nesanovich

COLORS OF THE RIVER
Stella Ann Nesanovich

First Edition
December 2015

ISBN: 978-1-329-68125-5

Yellow Flag Press
224 Melody Drive
Lafayette, LA 70503

www.yellowflagpress.com

YFP-132

Acknowledgments

Grateful acknowledgment is made to the publishers of the following publications, in which the poems mentioned first appeared, some in slightly different form or under a different title.

Anglican Theological Review: "St. Leo's," as "The Churches of My Youth," "T.S. Eliot at Norwich," "Shakespeare After London"

The Christian Century: "Beach Pictures, 1954," "The Feast of All Souls," "Sorrow Stalks Me in an Old Coat"

Christianity and Literature: "The Dead Return" as "A Familiar Face"

Chronicles: A Magazine of American Culture: "Home Fires," "Evening," "Sligo—Yeats Summer School, 1968," "We Talk of Flowers, Rocks, Earth," "Returning from New Mexico," "Passage," "A Talisman Against Falling"

Hurricane Blues: Poems about Katrina and Rita (Southwest Missouri State University Press): "The Sinking of New Orleans"

Journal of College Writing Reflections—Writing the Blues: "The Streets of New Orleans"

2005 Jubilee Anthology: "For Leo in April"

2008 Jubilee Anthology: "Revisiting New Orleans in a Season of Joy"

Louisiana English Journal: "Through the Looking Glass," "Childhood Places"

Louisiana Literature: "The Ache," "Café du Monde," "The Colors of the River," Oyster Shuckers," "Mark Hewitt's Pottery," "Turning Toward Home"

The Louisiana Review: "Childhood Places," "Scattering My Sister's Ashes"

The MacGuffin: "Michelangelo Supervises the Cutting of Marble"

Magnolia Quarterly: "Through the Looking Glass"

Modern Age: "T.S. Eliot at Norwich"

My Father's Voice (Yellow Flag Press): "Rubella"

My Mother's Breath (Chicory Bloom Press): "Childhood Places"

Rougarou: "Return to the House of Memories," "The Day of the Dead Draws Near" as "In Paradisum"

Shadow and Light: A Literary Anthology on Memory (Peterborough, New Hampshire): "Keepers of Memory"

The Southern Poetry Anthology IV: Louisiana (Texas Review Press): "Oyster Shuckers," "Revisiting New Orleans in a Season of Joy"

Swamp Lily Review: "The Batture," "On Icons," "The Colors of the River"

Third Wednesday: "Winter"

Vineyards: A Journal of Christian Poetry (on-line): "Returning to Grand Coteau"

Vision/Verse 2009-2013: An Anthology of Poetry (Yellow Flag Press): "Breaking the Surface," "Agrigento," "Tree Men," "The Colors of the River"; "On Icons"

Words, Words, Words: "For Leo in April"

2011 Writers' Conference Anthology: Tree Men"

Table of Contents

I.   8

Breaking the Surface   9
Childhood Places   10
Rubella   11
Oyster Shuckers   12
St. Leo's   13
Beach Pictures, 1954   14
Café du Monde   15
Home Fires   16
The Sinking of New Orleans   17
A Childhood Lately Understood   18

II.   20

Keepers of Memory   21
The Bottom of the Cup Tea Room   22
Homemade Muffulettas   24
The Dead Return   25
On Icons   26
Pitot House   27
Evening   28
Winter   29
Scattering My Sister's Ashes   30
For Leo in April   32
The Feast of All Souls   34

III.   35

Michelangelo Supervises the Cutting of Marble   36
Shakespeare After London   37
T.S. Eliot at Norwich   38
Agrigento   41

Sligo—Yeats Summer School, 1968   42
Today, a Tapestry Spun with Gold   43
We Talk of Flowers, Rocks, Earth   45
Returning from New Mexico   46
August Aubade   47
The Day of the Dead Draws Near   48
Through the Looking Glass   49
Mark Hewitt's Pottery   50
Passage: After Seeing a Photograph of the Himalayas   51

IV.   52

Return to the House of Memories   53
A Talisman Against Falling   54
The Ache   55
Sorrow Stalks Me in an Old Coat   56
The Streets of New Orleans   57
The Batture   58
Returning to Grand Coteau   59
Turning Toward Home   61
Wind Turbines   62
Tree Men   63
Revisiting New Orleans in a Season of Joy   64
The Colors of the River   66

Colors of the River: Poems

"So I find words I never thought to speak

In streets I never thought I should revisit…"

T.S. Eliot, "Little Gidding," *Four Quartets*

I.

Breaking the Surface

After Chris Marcello's painting, *Making More Waves*

She speaks to us of memory,
this fragile girl before a crimson sky.
Amid silver swirls of water, her arms mirror
sun's rays striking disks of light.

She wades in depths of fire-rimmed whirls
and radiant circles, stirring an aura
of the past, autumn landscape,
and mind's slow tidal flow in time.

Easy here to wade into a pool of dreams,
their gauze-thin shimmer like luminous
streams ferrying us to our youth.

Childhood Places

They were permanent, eternal as God,
people and places I didn't question
and never imagined vanishing.

I would always be susceptible to others' whims—
my parents forever young, my siblings beside me.
Every Christmas a year's distance, sorrow a transient

shower. Toasty mornings, light sparkling
in a mirror gilded with flowers, I find
a tricycle as gift, a silky sea blue I love.

On a beach, my mother and I trudge
toward Cape San Blas. Eight years old,
I am sunburned, the moment intense as fire.

In memory's castle, landscapes
remain, rich as jacquard satin.

Rubella

On the margins of memory:
blinds drawn to prevent eye damage,
sunlight filtered through lattice.
My father is home with me,
clips paper dolls for his youngest,
the one he dubbed "Duckle Dunn."

The men in my family possessed
that gift of naming, like Adam
in the first garden mouthing "bee,"
"apple," "serpent," and "Eve."
Words slid on their tongues as smoothly
as water or honey, a love of words
passed to me when a child,
thrilled with the slim ballerinas
my father trimmed for me
years ago in a darkened room.

Oyster Shuckers

Their names are no longer familiar.
There was Mack and Sleepy and Claude,
at whose home I spent hours.
My brother must remind me about Eviste,
Lucius, and August, the one who ate
only bananas for lunch and napped
on the concrete floor of my father's shop.

Once he told a woman the oysters
weren't good, unsalty and too small.
She was stupid, he said, to purchase
oysters like that.

Vanished now, with the oyster dressing
made from New Orleans French bread,
airy and light, and the Fridays
when my father brought home
a pint to dip in cornmeal and fry—
oysters the shuckers had opened.

St. Leo's

Always stained glass: amethyst, vermilion,
blue and emerald, sun-brightened saints,
scenes from Our Savior's life or the Virgin's,
windows depicting Eve and the serpent,
the leaden lines visible only from without.

Carved statues and the stations, Simon
helping Jesus, Veronica to wipe His face.
Golden tabernacles for the body of Christ,
rounded doors etched in filigree
to signify ineffable mystery.

The courtyard of St. Leo's held a grotto
where candles danced in claret wells,
filled triple tiers to honor Mary,
forever cloaked in white and blue.
I would attend early Mass, return
afternoons to keep vigil, pray
novenas for causes I cannot recall.

Whatever my sorrow, my desire,
spirits lifted with Eucharist,
censed during Benediction:
haze of myrrh across the nave,
words and song graced by Latin.

Beach Pictures, 1954

The stamp on the backs reads July 12th,
photos faded to green
ripening to sepia edges.
Only reds are vivid. The sea grays
to a dark line marking the sky.

Aunt Thelma and Uncle Dimps stand on dunes
scattered with sea oats, her towel limp
against a thigh, the flounce of her suit.

Joy studies the sand. I etch something
in the air, my hair a tousled wedge.
Mother tucks legs for the pose.

In another, my aunt grasps my sister's arm—
Laurene, the first to die. Two of us
lock arms, stoop when waves break.

Laurene stands alone, already separating herself.

Café du Monde

Summer, a night when we have pleaded
for beignets, crisp triangles sprinkled
with powdered sugar, heavy when cooled,
mottling paper with oily circles.
Café du Monde: car windows down, warm air glazing
our arms with sweat, glistening from my father's
tattoo, the horseshoe reading "Mother."
The glare of city lights mapping streets,
neon patterns of the old Quarter with its wet bricks,
the hum of cicadas, circular pillars.
Beyond, the levee, the river.

Hunch-backed Buicks and Chevrolets
diagonally park as waiters arrive
toting trays of doughnuts and *café au lait*,
richly flavored with scalded milk
like the first sweet inhalation of sugar
spinning up with our breath,
powdering our fingers and hands
as we glide into that sensuous taste
of the past. I am eleven, just old enough
to know what I want, thinking

this moment will last, the sweet delight
will hold us forever: my sister and me,
the black Hudson with its dusky interior,
the smells from the docks and the river,
the fruit stands where Angelo sells my father
cantaloupes and peaches, and we have years
to plan, to dream, to bite into the hot flesh of life
with its tingle, its flavor, its promise.

Home Fires

Tenders of a fiery circle,
long before laws prohibited
backyard incinerations,
we children, city dwellers,
guarded perimeters
of our homespun blazes.

Stacks of newspapers and bills
spiraled and curled, folding in
on themselves like a lady's fan
closed with a snap of her wrist.

We poured water on embers
or buried the cinders until later,
when memory ignited new fires.

The Sinking of New Orleans

This is the doomsday manual for the city you love:
antique buildings where you schooled, lush green
landscapes, and Canal Street where you shopped,
bearing pedestrians in thigh-high water.

Bienville's town, doomed since its founding,
a delta with houses like hyacinths perched
on verdant petals, a city forever needing
prayers to St. Jude, divine intercession.

Dryades, street of forest nymphs, neighborhoods
honoring the Muses, Marigny and Bywater:
sunk and watered. A thousand dead at least,
unable to escape on clotted roads.

Some stayed for pets or precious mementos,
Aunt Bessie's pearls, photographs warped
by rain before the lake shatters levee walls,
bones of ancestors float from graves.

(Futile your plans for ashes interred with theirs.)
Raised cottages in the Ninth Ward cannot
resist the steady seeping; the old streets
curl about the river, the lake,

like a friend's betraying tongue licking
the sides of houses, chewing off paint,
gnawing the cedar beams of old estates,
for hurricanes do not respect place,

do not swerve for history's sake,
follow relentlessly the old slave routes.

A Childhood Lately Understood

Our parents scared us with stories
of rape, even while shells exploded
at home: electricity cut off,
and the phone, the landlord like a wolf
at the door. An inevitable truth:
childhood trauma surfaces late.

It was the tale of my late
sister Joy. Dying, she told the story
of a family friend, a drunk, in truth,
who abused her, exploding
nova before me, memories of wolves
I had known as well, cut off

from a painful past. Why did I cut off
my nails, toss my mother's gifts lately
into the trash? Who was the wolf
that devoured my childhood, whose story
appeased while he explored my body, exploded
the myth of innocence? Truth

is a tapestry woven of many-colored threads, some true-
hued; others clashing, mismatched, confusing. Cut-off
now from family, my sisters dead, memory explodes
with painful and graphic detail surfacing late.
Sexual ploys, unwanted French kisses, stories
of drunkenness growl like a hungry wolf

for the truth. What lamb lost her life to a wolf,
a thieving wolf who cared little for truth
or the girl child surviving his lies and stories,
her early arousal? She was cut off
forever from innocence, knew shame. Too late
to lament these offenses now. Virtue explodes

like a nova, a shooting star exploding
the innocence we expect in children, for wolves
will feed their needs, ignore others'. Too late
for them to worry who was harmed, the truth
of childhood destroyed or cut off,
the heroine smothered within her own story.

Every child likes stories, likes explosive
endings, nothing cut off for the hero, and the wolf
brought to face the truth, when wisdom arrives late.

II.

Keepers of Memory

Outside the circle of chiefs and braves
talking of paths the tribe must take,
who will fight, who linger, the women
listen, record treaties in memory's ledgers,
the patterns of seasons, claims made in trade.
They carry the past, like the children
corded to their backs. No written words
to recall their knowledge, their stories:
how to build a fire from scrap wood,
the buffalo's offspring and mate,
histories of diseases and deaths,
the losses in childbirth, the years of drought.
And after the winter snows, the heart's history
of rejoicing in prairies of clover.

The Bottom of the Cup Tea Room

Details like pebbles on a tide-washed shore:
the palm reader's shawl, small sandwiches,
iced tea in tall glasses, a Tarot deck,
the hand that held mine.

At thirteen I did not know of Julia,
the tearoom's ghost, haunting where she once lived.
Years on, I learned her story:
how this octoroon mistress of a white lover
was found on the roof, her nude body
forever stilled in December dark.

Infatuated with an ex-marine,
whose arms vined with dragon tattoos
snaking in shades of red and blue,
my love would fade over time,
a kinder fate than Julia's.
Her dusky skin prohibited
miscegenation, yet she begged
her lover to break the *code noir*
while he, in jest, promised to wed her
if she strode naked on the roof
all evening in cold weather.

Exotic as the old city, the legend
is retold with sightings of a girl
on a roof in the French Quarter.
Police arrive to rescue an apparition,
find only vapors from the river.

*

Fifty years since my visit,
I still recall the fortune-teller's words.
Like Julia's ghost, I cling to hope
and remember how I sought a sign,
elusive as beads fallen from a string of pearls.

Homemade Muffulettas

Saturdays in summer my father
brought home ingredients fresh
from Central Grocery on Decatur:

two kinds of Italian bread—
braided and sprinkled with sesame seeds;
the other, flat and round.

There were jars of oil-soaked salad
rich with black Kalamata
and green pimento-stuffed olives,
capers, and giardiniera.

On thick slices of bread
we layered provolone,
Genoa salami, mortadella,
ham, and mozzarella
and topped the tiers
with olive salad.

Leftover bread never
lasted—I would tear
the braids apart,

dip them in olive oil,
mortadella and pepperoncini

flavoring my memory.

The Dead Return

I have seen them, know the dead return:
ancestral stars visible in dreams,
luminaries present in a lingering scent,
someone long passed, nearby in a room,
seated in a wingback chair or at a desk.
Years after their deaths, they visit,
young and vibrant, alluring as Venus
rising on a cloudless night. Once
my grandfather's photograph surfaced
in a book—everywhere I glimpsed
that familiar face, his dark suit, the furled
umbrella he always carried. Perhaps
he called my name, like the gardener
to Magdalene, come to anoint his flesh.

On Icons

After Karen Wink's photograph *Tin Man*

A myth aloft like film in wind,
two Tin Men dangle in a cloudless sky.

Creator, director, the artist revels
in his design: facial furrows

and a smile to mirror the shadow
whose twin with painted grin

and shoe-button eyes dances within
the camera's lens. No plated cone

for the maker's head. Instead,
a tweed fedora, emblem of noted

coaches: Tom Landry of the Cowboys,
Bear Bryant with his Crimson Tide.

What hidden desire shimmers in sunlight,
what doppelganger so clearly dazzles?

Empty forms rattle in evening breezes,
awaiting the Wizard's ransom:

oil for creaky joints, and the welcomed
return of the Woodman's heart.

Pitot House

—New Orleans

A storm ripples Bayou St. John,
propels wind to bang gallery doors,
dampens the outdoor stairs,
the hard old cypress boards.

A Creole colonial home where banana trees,
a parlor garden, and circular stucco pillars
signal entry to another world,
here hours slip, measures fade.

Along the exterior galleries,
shutters shield us from spiraling rain.
French doors open toward the bayou,
shift breezes through high-ceilinged rooms.

Inside, we gaze on carved wooden mantels,
rich mahogany tables and chairs,
and study the portrait of a Creole woman,
whose image bears the weight
of lives well beyond two-hundred-years.

Rain lashes walls, shakes the branches
of lemon and Satsuma trees. Time distills
amid the steady drizzle, the robust blast
of wind along the bayou's frothy sides.

Evening

The dusk wheels up,
unfurls like moist fern:
only a glow of sunlight
west, a sliver of coral
like a lantern ascending
a distant hill, sweeping
a small path, a whiff
of flame over a ravine,
night's dense forest.

Cricket song, whirr
of bat wing—distance
masked by shade,
an ebony blanket
of sky. Moonlight
the only currency
to buy us passage
before slumber,
tether to our dreams.

Winter

January's bitter chill
when the old cat has died,
mirror of my soul's
discontent—unease
at fractured plans:
no trip to lessen the ache
of joints, pained spine.

Yet in the kitchen window,
warmed by western sun,
a paper-white hyacinth
offers its sweet scent,
lightens the heart:
a gift to counter
the stagnant frost
and winter's remote,
cold moon.

Scattering My Sister's Ashes

September 23, 2005, Lake Charles, Louisiana

White as sawdust bleached by the sun,
shards of calcium, the lake's brown milk—
not the resting place she had chosen,
an Alpine village, Bavaria's crest. Here
a broken sack of bone and ash dusting
my hands, Katrina's tide unhinging minds
and the small box that held her remains.

A curious fish visits where we stand,
the seawall her mausoleum. Her husband
crosses himself and weeps. So much has
interfered with her wish: the dissolution
of the Twin Towers, new restrictions
on travel, certainly with her casket.
My brother-in-law, a registered alien

and Green Card holder, feared arrest.
Germany, he said, did not allow such transport.
Everything now would be searched, perhaps
the reliquary itself unbound and her last home
concrete floors, the terminal her end,
not the hillside she envisioned and hoped
to remain when winter's snows came.

Days after her scattering, Hurricane Rita
surged through the city, washing the shore
where she was cast—but perhaps her ashes
had already sunk to the depths of whatever
force brews these storms. Perhaps
she had already been carried to the Gulf,
distilled beneath brine and kelp, or

spilled on a distant land she visited once:
Guatemala, Antigua, Puerto Rico—those years
lost in memory's seas. The body comes down
to this: dust strewn on water, amniotic fluid
we lived in once. Submerged in ocean again,
we join the tidal cycle.

For Leo in April

1.

It is as if one hundred years have passed.
I am back at my desk, grading papers,
Preparing lectures, aware of your absence
From these halls, how you will never again
Come to my office for peppermints and talk,
Or walk near the oaks and azaleas wreathing
The campus. I think of the Auden poem
You always cited at such times of loss,
How the Old Masters were never wrong
About suffering, how life goes on,
Demanding everyday tasks: classes
To teach, students to counsel,
Tasks you performed with skill.

2.

All my life birds have signaled transformation,
So the day you died when crows hovered
In the street before my car, unhastened
By the turning ignition, I knew their
Transfiguring sign. Today, another sign:
A dove alighting on the Cathedral steeple
As your casket was borne through the doors.
Family and friends, deeply mourning,
Gasped at that presence atop the cross.

3.

These are some things I remember:
Our trips to Oxford, Shreveport, and Waco,
A floor-clearing twist at Sarah Cash's wedding,
zigzags of tar on the Texas highway

Bearing us to Baylor, the Browning Library.
Dinner and drinks with my sister and her husband
At Sweet Basil's in New Orleans,
Countless poetry readings together,
And meals at the Crab Palace, martinis
Beforehand—you comfortable in my rocker—
Our last trip to Thibodaux, your gift Palm Sunday
Past of burying my old cat Keela.

4.

In the serene music accompanying
Your funeral, I pictured your life
A pentacle mosaic, points of gold
Radiating grace. Your friend, I am
A small stone, tessera really,
Illumined by your wisdom and love.

The Feast of All Souls

November 2

The dead visited this morning: sisters,
parents, aunts and uncles, old professors
and friends--faces so vivid they again
appeared in my room through memory's lens.

Did families stage a yard sale later
in the Catholic cemetery on Common,
a table set up in the center, orange water
cooler in view? But I am mistaken.

It's All Souls Day when people assemble
to clean the crumbling graves and to honor
their dead, whose remnant bones sometimes tumble
from ancient crypts, although their souls have soared

like skeins of starlings, whose sudden flight
in sunlight dyes wings a shimmer of white.

III.

Michelangelo Supervises the Cutting of Marble

That deep blue vein tells me where to chisel,
How to free my Lazarus from his linen tomb.
This piece carries a sword hilt. See
The warrior already turning to sever
His foe's head. His enemy, unlucky fellow,
Claws like a vine against the sky, smoke
Trails in autumn. Mary's breast was easy:
The marble offered a blush of milky flesh.
All stone boasts a figure within,
Fertile with grace, awaiting birth.

Shakespeare After London

"Shakespeare had actually retired from the theatre and spent some
years as a lay minister in the parish close to where he grew up…"
—Michael McGirr, *Things You Get for Free*

Parson Will reads Scripture every Sunday
long after London, the theatrical farce
and creative spark. Here in Stratford,
near where he schooled, the quiet lane
where the children and Anne remained,
he passes the plate, offers his wisdom
to those who would bolt from kids and spouse,
take the nursemaid in the bower for sport
an hour, pinch the salt—who'd be looking?

He had seen all sorts of folly at the Rose,
long before the King's Men and the Globe.
He knew human foibles, pride and lust,
princely arrogance. What could he say
in cleric's garb to sway them from sin,
the rifling desire to taste pleasures they
fancied sated him?   Hadn't he come back,
the sot turned from his sack, chiding them
with Nehemiah, Jonah, minor prophets?
London could beguile, but let the garden
serve as symbol: festive beauty does not linger,
and kale, harvested daily, will fill a larder.

He will be buried here, he knows,
amid the tumble of old stones.
Cousin Michael's bones nearby,
other kin in decaying tombs.
Better to rest in the village of one's birth
than strut a foreign stage at death.
The logic of life charts a grand circle.

T.S. Eliot at Norwich

1942

Swirl and riddle beyond the gray wall
where she was anchored, an old church,
a labyrinth of vines and dragonflies now,
maze of thistles overtaking enclosures,
crevices and crenellations of vegetation,
tufts of grass piercing hermitage
and cloistered cell. Her every choice
renunciation, her fame transcendent.

A river ripples against a bank,
her wisdom flooding the years so we,
in our desolate century, imprisoned
and starved for sanctity, encounter
her visions and devotion, how she assigned
no blame for sin, let shine as sterling
God's love of all who came to call
and lingered near the water's edge.

From such inhabitude of solitude
she spoke a truth as only sages can,
knowing the heart's most secret cries.
A red candle now praises yellowed stone,
flames to comfort the frightened spirit,
hearing again the gunners near the coast,
picturing in this pastoral place
the London fires, the missile's shrill voice.

Rank smell of mussels from the river,
the dark, cold, empty desolation
of those *vast waters* not far
from where she walked. Leper houses
once clustered about these church walls,
embraced the town gates. The rattle

of warning clappers stirs in imagination:
through the small squint, the narrow

space at ground where those accursed
were fed the holy word, the Lord
as blessed bread—that part Julian chose,
a garden enclosure like the soul
awash in God's emboldening love.
Now a crumbling grindstone, smoky glass
lie amid old elms and fallen timbers.
Yet all manner of thing shall be well.

I saved her words for the last Quartet,
the final movement in symphonic work,
casting the soul's pilgrimage in verse
to quiver like spring on earth, alive
and beating, discharging all, myself no less,
from sin and error—or so I hoped.
I thought the Greeks my masters once,
struck redemptive gold in sacrament.

What do we know of her in that small cell
at window where she heard some confess
to crimes they dared not tell the priest?
Nourishment on desolate nights, her life
a bended knee embraced by words
transcending place, this very poem.
A gray figure offering sense for dreams,
the correlation of journey and loss.

Autumn afternoon, secluded chapel,
half ruins now, scaffolding for thoughts
echoing in my heart, quick as the fire
of grace. Here a bronze crucifix twisted
by heat, a scent of apples, shocked grain,
perhaps an end and a beginning,
The cycles spinning, the slate of years
unchanged in rural places beyond these walls.

Agrigento

After Chris Marcello's painting *Valle dei Templi*

Agrigento: the word spins and swirls
about the tongue. Gods strode here,
wandered sienna rocks to the sea
below the scarp, a site for Divinity
centuries before Christ.

Soul speaks in myriad voices. Citizens
of Akragas prayed in dithyrambic chant
to mighty Hera, fiery Vulcan, muscled
Hercules, Olympian Zeus.

Azure sky, a darker sea rise beyond worn
and spacious stairs, skirted now by column
remnants, pillars from an era alien to our own.
A lone cypress in the distance, wind-weathered
greenery flanking stones as we mount,
breathe freely salt air.

Demeter, Persephone, Asclepius:
we yearn to dance within your temples,
to know the ecstasy of worshipers
whose faith brewed elixirs worthy
of a god to heal countless ills,
others to fashion the seasons,
or hurl lightning and wield thunder.

Sligo—Yeats Summer School, 1968

Black-faced sheep graze meadows near
the grammar school where your room
sits in a tower and morning light reveals
distant hills of Donegal, the Garavogue River
below your window. Lough Gill lies east,
Ben Bulben's mountain face a few miles more.

A week late for this gathering, you missed
the planned tours, but Lydia, the housemother,
born in India of parents in British service,
drives you in her Morris Minor
to the Lake Isle of Innisfree, beyond
to Drumcliff Churchyard, where Yeats is laid:
a single rose rests against the limestone.

You dine with your professor and his wife
in Ballisodare, home to Yeats' ancestors,
the Pollexfens. The school's closing
evening, a party with young Irish dancers
and a harpist. An old jokester urges a shot
of whiskey, a chaser of Guinness stout.

The next morning on a train to Dublin,
you recall the story an old priest told—
one you would repeat to your students:
a legend of the sidhe, mythic horsemen
who pass from Donegal across the green
below Ben Bulben—a plea to leave
unscathed the poet's grave.

Today, A Tapestry Spun with Gold

memory melding places I have traveled
 into one weave: the glowing yellow-
  painted grill in Brownsville, Oregon,
   and Mikee's Seafood Emporium
in Gulf Shores. The calm Gulf exchanges
 currents with the craggy northern Pacific,
  while gulls and murres of Cape Perpetua
   resemble the spindle-legged plovers
pecking seaweed on Alabama's shores.
 I have seen such gulls roosting near home
  as well, K-Mart's lot a refuge in storms.

At the Mobile Museum of Art tucked
 near Springhill and the city park,
  the Dürer prints of Christ's passion,
   the saints, and mythical figures,
etched in fine detail, turn my thoughts
 back to Munich's Alte Pinakothek.

Thirty years ago I traveled with a friend
 from London to Ostend, Rotterdam
  and Amsterdam. We sailed the Rhine
   to Mainz, visited Heidelberg, then
  Munich.
Touring the museum, we spent hours
 before the Dürers and Ruebens,
  ate Leberkäse in the train station,
   later dined on beer and Sauerbraten.

Here in Gulf Shores, Mikee's offers
 mainly fried seafood and onion rings,
  culinary feasts far from German fare
   or English tea scones at Lyons.

How is it memory melds so many places
      into one, as if life's journeys threaded
           together in the end, creating a single
                 weave, a textile of panels pressed
together, a shift in landscape evocative of the past?

We Talk of Flowers, Rocks, Earth

Guadalupe Mesa, New Mexico, 2009

Leaves of one plant resemble praying hands.
A thin cross takes shape on an adobe wall.
Crowned by scarab wings, it looms
as haggard as St. Dymphna's severed head.

At lunch, we talk of flowers, rocks, and earth:
desert landscape with red-hot poker caressed
by crimson petals, slender lavender
beside the vibrant juniper and yarrow.

Later, I find a hinged rock, knee-shaped,
to mirror my arthritic pain: a signature
smoothed by rain, nature's baptism.

Some mornings, we see a luminous
form on the mesa's side: the Virgin
for whom the butte is named.

Winds shimmer as if possessed
by jeweled feet dancing to the sun's
steep rise, the earth as Eucharist.

Returning from New Mexico

Well southeast of the Sangre de Cristo,
the arroyos of the desert and starkness
of White Sands, the Texas Panhandle's
wind turbines and tornado shelters,
I awaken to the cooing of gray doves
along the coastal plain and land level
to the bayou's edge—pecan, live oak,
and cypress near sheaths of sugar cane.

Cattle egrets wheel up from flooded fields,
rice spirals from pools, as turtles amble
across roadways—the lush green an emblem
of renewal, this variance of landscape
a metaphor for creation, a world
translucent as crystal beads, resonant
as the chant of monks, praying the Hours,
ancient demarcation of the seasons.

August Aubade

Light breezes cool my skin
as skies brighten to coral
and vestiges of mist linger
before sun's full rise.

A lover amid sweet flora,
the soft scent of rose petals,
the sparrows' morning psalms,
I hover over blueberry bushes,

hunt plump, ripe berries knotted
in clusters, floribunda deep
within winged branches,
orbs like distant blue stars.

The Day of the Dead Draws Near

Cusp of autumn curves into winter
as weather cools this morning,
and snow pelts the Northeast
before Halloween. The Day
of the Dead draws near.

In the cemeteries of New Orleans
and the Cajun prairies, families
bring chrysanthemums, scour headstones
and walled crypts. Along Cane River,
candles will fill the night, adorn
whitewashed wooden markers of the poor,
daubed with painted names of their dead.

The ashes of my sisters are scattered
to waters here and abroad, while my parents
rest within a mausoleum. Nearby, remains
of grandparents, uncles, and cousins
lie entombed above the low water table.

I will not polish marble plates or bear
fresh flowers on All Souls Day.
This Sunday, as the church year shifts
closer to Advent, I eat bread,
a Swedish rye censed with yeast.

Through the Looking Glass

We find ourselves in a strange new world,
sense we have climbed into a rabbit hole,
where small rooms lie hidden under rafters,
roofline aslant above washbasins,
intrigue supported by shelves of books.
Sunlight suffuses one bed at dawn,
a full moon frosts the other at dusk.
La Luna may alter our wits, render us
loco by morning, as our mothers warned.
Yet here we welcome a needed rest,
enjoy the refuge for hummingbirds and deer
visiting the yard and feeding quite near.
Days upended, our evening ripens under branches,
moonlight moving silently among our voices.

Mark Hewitt Pottery Exhibit

Ogden Museum of Southern Art, New Orleans

Wood-fired in a vast kiln,
in pebbly black, blue, green,
and amber glazes, they signal
humorous and solemn moods.

"Grandpa's" perforated crown
forms a giant saltshaker.
"Nunc Dimittis" honors
St. Simeon's prayer,
epitaph for one interred
within a blackened urn.

Bulbous jardinières, obelisks,
onion-domes, and burial urns
aligned on rectangular bases
in ritual procession,
they make gifts to the gods
in a pharaoh's tomb,
a sacred mausoleum
where I might kneel.

Passage:
After Seeing a Photograph of the Himalayas

Ridges of blue companions to clouds,
mountains smoked with white mists,
juxtaposition of earth and thin body:
transient flesh prey to gravity's pull.

In the photograph of Posang Pass,
against foothills of the world's highest places,
my friend dwarfs and changes.

How did she come to this passage?
What prayers did she offer this morning,
what blessings request for the day's trek?

Though my journey was pilgrimage
played on local stages, I heard
the soul's voice, learned its language and call.

Still, the small figure beckons
from mysteries older than language,
rising before we named them
Annapurna, Chomolungma, Himal Ganesh.

IV.

Return to the House of Memories

"Our soul is an abode."
        —Gaston Bachelard, *The Poetics of Space*

"I walk from region to region of my soul and I discover
that I am a bombed city."
        —Thomas Merton, *Journals*, March 3, 1953

One room has filtered light, the other darkness.
After years, I return to the house of memories.
Have I come at last to know who I am,
what manner of woman? In the time
I have been given, Sunday's child,
have I found a fragment to cherish?

On the street where I was born, jazz now
echoes from Snug Harbor, restaurants offer
the pleasure of rich seafood dishes.
Amid this shifting light, the sun sets the river
ablaze—glimpsed through a window, I sense
a current, partly hidden, endless changing.

First the years when suffering wielded its sword:
the dark weight of a pendulum pressing
my frame, deaths of sisters, luminous
in the end. Is the image I search for buried
in wreckage? What other veneer must I strip
before turning to the wood on the stair?

A Talisman Against Falling

It must be a spirit that catches you,
keeps you from falling, stumbling
toward the ledge of tall buildings,
lifts you after tripping face forward
on rugs in halls, sunken living rooms,
upending tables and lamps.

Perhaps it is fear itself that cautions:
avoid elevator shafts, high expressways,
mountain roads coiling like kites
toward heaven. High up, dizziness
begins, spins out of control. Your fall
will break circuits of trees, chevroned leaves
like cascading walls unblocking descent.

An unbalanced element of earth, some say
and urge crawling to steady your vision.
It's the sky, you want to tell them:
its limitlessness and endless promise,
and the sudden nudge to jump from heights.
Haven't you felt it, the desire to leap?
Sweet earth beckons, pulls you to her bosom,
pushes you forward with grace. She wishes
you knew the rapture she offers: salt and brine
of water-fringed beaches, damp, yielding sand.

The Ache

What is it I taste? Cardamom? Gumbo
with thyme and bay leaf? A musical note
plays on the edge of memory, swirls
into an abyss. Absence of roots, tendrils
adrift, once tied to a funky place:
antique green streetcars rumbling
down an oak-laden street, sweltering
summers, jazz, and beignets.

Home: rich with magnolias, sweet olive,
bougainvillea, crape myrtles, and wisteria.
The past like a melody I cannot retrieve
sways out of reach. I grasp for notes,
for phrases: phantoms like the spice
I cannot name.

Sorrow Stalks Me in an Old Coat

the color of churned water.
I have worn it for years—it
no longer fits, tugs at the waist
where I have grown under cover,
spreading like roots, like grief,
swelling in rows of deep rhizomes
long after sowing. How often
can a heart break? When
might I be rid of this old coat?

The Streets of New Orleans

—On seeing the flooding after Hurricane Katrina

Thirty years after departing
the stucco house in Gentilly,
for a moment this morning
chatter ceased, an internal
space opened, like the stillness
when a dog's bark ceases.

A child, I lived near an avenue
called St. Bernard in that city
with magical names, where saints
and muses share equal billing.
In that still space a sensuous flood:
the bricks of the Vieux Carré,

odors of molasses and coffee,
the chug of ships on the dark mix
of the Mississippi, churning
toward some port far from the city
of my birth, my youth, that place
now even more water than earth.

The Batture

"The Mississippi never lies at rest. It roils…It moves south in
layers and whorls, like an uncoiling rope…"
   —John M. Barry, *Rising Tide*

Never a steady velocity, like life's rough courses,
the river rises each spring, races downstream
toward New Orleans and the Gulf. Awakened
with the surge of melted snow, it vibrates
as if alive, like Lazarus roused from his tomb,
uncoiled from his winding sheet.

Beyond the roiling and the levee, between the river
and the mounds of cement and soil that imprison
its path, lies the batture, that flat land flooded
with this spring's rising. I remember the times
as a child when I visited my cousin Herman,
a Dock Board patrolman on the river, watched
the whorls that lapped the old wharves.
More recent trips allowed views from a hotel
window: morning and evening ferry crossings,
as if the river charted every stage of my life.

The ash tree's blossoms have withered
in summer's heat while the river has receded
again, and the batture will thrive once more
with new growth: thistle and palmetto,
wild iris, scrub oak, and river birch.

Returning to Grand Coteau

The last time, it was summer with tiers
of honeyed wheat, robes of iridescence
from live oak canopies. This autumn
we dine at Catahoula's. Photographs
of Catahoula hounds with leopard spots
and two-toned eyes line the walls.
Rich French foods, flavored to perfection,
sate our desires: chicken-sausage gumbo
in a roux-base, tender green onions
as garnish. My friend orders mushroom
crepes with grilled asparagus. I request pasta
in creamy wine sauce with shrimp,
sun-dried tomatoes, and artichoke hearts.
We imbibe artisan beer brewed from pecans,
and white wine. After the bread pudding,
we walk to antique stores and the Kitchen Shop,
then the grounds of St. Charles College,
where memories of my many Advent retreats
flood back, the gray December drizzle
stirred in a heavy brew of grief amid prayer.

I recount tales of the nun who scolded me
for writing, the old priest who praised
my poems, and Sister Pat, the artist,
who took me to the unused third floor
under a turreted roof with rows
of small chapels. Windows opened
to a view of all Grand Coteau,
the Interstate to Lafayette and beyond.
With clay she gave me, I molded
a woman newly born from earth.

Other memories surface past the grotto
to Our Lady of Lourdes and the old graveyard
that always beckons. Once, I fell asleep
on a bench and thought I heard the dead speak:
the early Jesuits taken by Yellow Fever,
Confederate soldiers from Louisiana infantry—
their graves now marked with rebel flags.
I weep again over my sister Joy's death,
the way her ashes spilled upon my hands.

We pause, rest on a large double tomb,
the husband buried long before,
the wife's side still unoccupied.
To the northeast, the coteau, the ridge
of land above the flat Gulf prairies:
hay already bundled and baled
where Black Angus dot the rise.

Turning Toward Home

Mandeville to New Orleans

After a day of soup and quiche
we turned south toward home,
a coral sun and lavender clouds
rising over the velvet dark lake,
like the future we rode toward,
silent as spans of the cantilevered
bridge before us, its golden lights
twin starships seeking Earth.

Beneath us, water moved
like memory's current casting
me again on the river, riding
the ferry over that muddy track
through marsh and city, once more
inspired to sing as wind stirred
my hair and heartbreak passed
far beyond the Gulf Stream.

Wind Turbines

If these were trees,
aliens planted them,
filled the plains
far as sight reaches,
gleaming white metal
in day, orange vapor
lamps luminous at night
stretching to the deep
cobalt world of stars.

If I could move so,
arms spread to embrace
the wind, the Spirit
whirling around me,
I would know
something of heaven,
how it rises suddenly
from earth, radiant,
toward vast mystery.

Tree Men

We are feasting at the Napoleon House
on red beans and rice, a Reuben, Abita beer—
when out of the window appear
leaves and stalks of banana trees.

First glance suggests greenery on stilts,
the blurred vision of that fellow in Scripture
whose sight Jesus had to restore twice.

But it's two trash men rolling carts
with banana tree debris, folded
like crumbled pages in a waste can.
They wend their burden around the corner
to some unseen compost or dumpster.

Later, over shared desserts of bread pudding
and cannoli, I see them again: bins
filled with banana leavings,
a second round of dissecting
and hauling from some hidden courtyard,
a foraged place behind Quarter walls.

I would leap from my chair, spurred by a rich brew
of Creole coffee and my heady desire
for a New Orleans garden at my Lake Charles home,
but I am miles away and know these shearings
will not thrive in a less tropical climate.

You wave a hand near my face, call me
from reverie. Then I remember
the Shumard oak you planted in Houston,
grown tall and healthy, unscathed by storms.

Revisiting New Orleans in a Season of Joy

"I knew I had to come home. It was a matter of time."
—Mona Lisa Saloy, *The Times Picayune*,
December 26, 2007

I

How could I forget the rooflines of tile,
the details of plaster gargoyles embracing
interior walls? Seven years scarred
with deaths and flood, and I am home again
amid these scenes and familiar scents,
the years peeling away my fears,
imagination's false claims. A sluice gate
opens to streams of tears and their sister joy.

Out Gentilly Boulevard past the ruins
of Elysian Fields, our stucco house appears
smaller than I recall. On Bruxelles off Broad
the grocery store my great uncle owned
has disappeared. Lakeside, the university
mushroomed, swelling structures everywhere.
I can no longer locate where I officed or schooled.
Only the mansions along St. Charles remain.
Memories rise like smoke of yesteryear.
I shiver and curl up against the cold.

II

Before the museum, the oaks have vanished,
replaced by slim stalks with auburn leaves.
Two exhibits depict the pain of Katrina,
Rolland Golden paintings and the art of children
displaced and lost, working their grief and fears
into crayon drawings. Frames of destruction
will play for years in their memory's films.

Amid pouring rain, a squadron of ducks
align at equidistant paces across the road.
A straight edge of blue bills to warn us
to flee before the waters again drown the city?
Is this how they acted when the levees broke
and the lake crafted her month-long tides?

III

Before and after, there is hope: in the Quarter,
at Café Degas, ripe with meals to tempt the palate:
pompano with lemon-caper risotto, yam and tasso
soup, golden croissants and quiche, special treats
of coffee and beignets. Pleasures of the tongue
and flesh, of friendship renewed, recumbent
as leaves folded by winds, lifting us beyond
what we believe we know or understand.

The Colors of the River

New Orleans

Dawn light shimmers like golden seams threading
mists of cobalt waves. Noon, silver peaks
rise above muddy brown. This morning, gray
monochrome of sky-cloud-river waked only
by a ship of brick red, another with tan
and turquoise hull. Barges hauling gravel
and oyster shells ply sleepily past, pushed
by snub-nosed tugs. A cruise liner
halves the river at its crescent,
bending beyond Algiers Point. Apogee
of afternoon marks a southern voyage—
skies already dusky with rain,
the air bright with tension, thunderstorms
mottling the river's spins and whirls.

Old friends and new, we gather to celebrate,
share meals and laughter, let stories
fill our hours as we ignore the fading
colors of sky and water. Ship whistles—
basso, profundo—caution passage.
Who speaks for the river pilots
or directs this traffic of barges, cargo,
and cruise liners? What *vanitas* painting
might capture shifts of shade, the candle
nearly extinguished? Who among us here,
dining on seafood and beer, will first depart?

About the Author

Dr. Stella Ann Nesanovich is the author of three chapbooks of poems: *A Brightness That Made My Soul Tremble: Poems on the Life of Hildegard of Bingen* (Blue Heron Press), *My Mother's Breath* (Chicory Bloom Press), and *My Father's Voice* (Yellow Flag Press)as well as a full-length collection, *Vespers at Mount Angel: Poems* (Xavier Review Press). Her poetry has appeared in *Uncommonplace: An Anthology of Contemporary Louisiana Poets* (LSU Press), Hurricane *Blues: Poems About Katrina and Rita* (Southwest Missouri State University Press), *Shadow and Light: A Literary Anthology on Memory* (The Monadnock Writers Group of New Hampshire) and *The Southern Poetry Anthology IV: Louisiana* (Texas Review Press). In 1999 she received an artist fellowship from the Louisiana Division of the Arts; in 2009 she was nominated for a Pushcart Prize. She is Professor Emerita of English from McNeese State University. Her website is Nesanovich.com